MY LORD BUDDHA
OF CARRAIG ÉANNA

Paddy Bushe

fa Gill,

hoping you'll come back to

see him again.

Beir beannacht,

Paddy

DEDALUS PRESS
DUBLIN, IRELAND

ACKNOWLEDGEMENTS

Acknowledgements are due to the editors of the following where a number of these poems originally appeared: *The SHOp, Cork Literary Review, Poetry Ireland Review, New Hibernia Review, Irish Pages* and *Puckerbrush Review,* and the online journals *Softblow, Southword, Manchester Review* and *The First Cut.* 'January' and 'Waiting' first appeared in *Shine On: Irish Writers for Shine* (Pat Boran, ed., Dedalus Press, 2011).

Most of the poems in Section IV were commissioned by the Office of Public Works and published in *Voices at the World's Edge: Irish Poets on Skellig Michael* (Paddy Bushe, ed., Dedalus Press, 2010).

for Pearse Hutchinson

Contents

I

Organ Recital, Norwich Cathedral

for John and Hilary Wakeman

The organ-pipes, sunstruck by the last rays
Through the high cathedral windows, beamed
Beyond sin or sanctity, radiating around
Arches, colonnades and flowering vaults.
And, secular with sacred, Latinate
With vernacular, the music moved
Eternally within the walls. Bede's sparrow
Would have flown in and never left.

And most vernacular of all, the organ-screen,
Arched high between the nave and choir,
Came down to earth on the digital screen
Where the organist's fingers spread wide
Over keyboards, and bellows and stops.
How *digital* and *screen* revelled in all this,
This playing hide-and-seek with meaning,
This waltz, this *benedictus de profundis!*

And for no reason except all this, I recalled
That afternoon's walk through the low arch
Into the herb garden, close by the cathedral,
Its sunny lines of aromatic, curative paths
Notated by bees, who'd pulled out all the stops,
Swelling *digitalis* into passages of fairy fingers,
Worts, sorrels, balms and alliums falling over
Themselves, dying to be useful again.

Milking Time in Ballyheigue

Since farmers knew that there is no such thing
As daylight saving, *wireless time* returned the hour
To *creamery time,* as I ran and was hoisted
To sit among churns, while wireless time
Was still harp-strings, startled to an aubade
Before the early morning news at eight.

And, down the waking street, the donkey drew
The slow swing of udders, the black and white
Processions towards milking, the warm ringing
Of milk in buckets, the cud of days chewed
Endlessly. All of this, in those unscythed summers
Before time coarsened, and radio news grew strident.

Breath

Although, downstream, the villagers were waiting
With open arms, garlands, and helping hands
To the landing, his raft refused the current
And drifted instead to the shallows.
And how inevitably it spun then,
Squeezing water through its thonged
And sinewed frame, and butted its way
Upstream, upwind, helplessly, a hooked fish
Ratcheting its way towards the reel!
And then the cave, the hoist, the entering
Through portal folds into that vast breath
Of familiar awe; how it enveloped him,
How brightly the veil lifted, lifted him high
And mighty through the fluted, opening roof!

Seeing the Pictures

for Bernard O'Donoghue

It all flickered back into my mind
When, at your reading, you recalled going
Not to a film, or cinema, but to *the pictures*
At whatever time it was, and when to leave
Was not decided by the final credits
Or any directorial cue, but by the whispered
I think that this is where we came in.
God knows, of course, it lacked all judgment.

And so, God knows, does this: how would it be
If the big picture always rolled out that way,
Freed from all that weight of ends and beginnings,
So that, recognising more or less your time,
While cigarettes glowed here and there in the dark
And smoke rose votively through projector beams,
You excused yourself past couples rearranging themselves
And slipped out, at the place where you came in?

Swans

I can't remember who, the other day,
Was on the phone, but I remember
Ever more clearly the two swans I saw

Through the sitting-room window, beating
Up from the estuary towards the lake,
Their stretch and span all urgent, all intent.

And by now, I think I can remember –
Despite the phone, the double-glazing –
The high whirring music of their wings

Building to a climax as they rose up
And over the gable, and the whole
House lifted, as if with filled sails.

The Etymology of Machias

for the Salt Coast Sages

Machias: bad little waterfall. And the falls
I stood by on my first morning in the town,
The river bellowing its brief, demented passage
Over and through the battered granite,
Would have whirled and turned and shredded
The birch-bark canoes of the Passamaquoddy
Who named and landmarked its clamour,
Paddling from the long silence of upriver.

The texture of the bark canoes lingered
In bankside trees, as pickups revved by,
And the calmer waters below remembered
The huge confusion of logs that careered
Over the falls, all that endless lumber
Of displacement, of clearance and re-naming
Floating downriver through good and bad places
Towards the schooners, their stirring sails.

Later, in the workshop, at the reading,
The poetry flowed. We climbed the falls
With our fragile, upturned canoes,
Nosed them up creeks of possibility,
Sent all of our lumber tumbling gloriously
Over the cascade, and sure-footed our way
To where the schooners' sails bulged
With a fair wind towards the open sea.

Machias. Not a bad little place at all.

The Search

He wanted to know what language the river
Spoke at its earliest bubblings, how the brown bog
Inflected its original accent, what gutturals

Were borrowed from the warning-calls of waders,
And if the waders' voices had carried traces
Of the great salty marsh from where they came.

He wanted to record the dialect of the stories
The mountain could recall only in colours
Ground, with auspicious words, from its earth.

Was it true, he wondered, that a wind
Skinning the stones of a gulley could aspirate
The initial syllables of a ritual curse?

He knew that nothing ever takes place
Until it has been told, and yet he searched
For a language antecedent to its words.

Was *hare* truly the diminutive of *deer*?
Rowan a synonym for *magic*? Did the heather
Trace its roots back to the articulacy of stone?

He thought he could detect, just, the unvoiced
Vowels wrapped tight in buds, the consonants
Which might bring to light the shooting leaves.

The falling tones of curlews, disyallabic
In the evening light, insisted that something
Needed to be said, but the words eluded him.

He hoped to catch and analyse the rhythms
Of sunlight through the birches as he walked,
The inbreath of wonder in lichens, in mosses.

And the salmon in the pool? Did wise words inhere
In the repetition of its scales, or seek utterance
In the silent vowel mouthed against the flow?

The elision of his footsteps through the leaf-mould
Was like prayer growing into mantra, himself
Taking the sacred air with the sibilant leaves above.

Abstract nouns he could hear, clearly pronounced,
But where they were spoken from or what it was
They were meant to convey was far beyond him.

So he walked deeper and wider into the land,
Catching now and then a strain of all these things
As he spoke, trying always to find the language

For what he still hoped he would sometime hear.

II

New Moon over Nepal

Over Himalayan foothills, on a scale
Inconceivable at home, a sickle moon rises
And edges itself against the grain of stars.

In the valleys, fluttering over the blue
Corrugated roofs, postered on flaking walls
Or sloganed in roadblocks and marches,

The hammer and sickle rises, on a scale
Inconceivable at home, and a king bows out
Amid talk of Maoist votes and landslides.

The Himalayan summits, which have seen
The other side of all of this before,
Feel their snow gather itself, and stiffen.

And they hold their breath, and listen,
Stock still, in the high, white silence.

Votary at Chaudaridara

for Pramita Timalsina

The early morning sun sheds light on the humps
And hollows of the water-buffalo's back, silvering

Those himalayan hips to pewter, inscribing
Its grey flanks with sutras in an old language

Fit for visitations. And so she comes, absorbed
In secret, four-year-old smiles the sun knows well.

Now her small fists unbunch, spreading orange light
As Pramita, radiant, offers marigolds to the buffalo.

Swing

for Prashant Timalsina

Everybody's feet, they say, should leave the earth
During *Dashain*, and walk the air like the kites
That spool themselves all over the expectant sky.

And so, as goats were brought in droves from hills,
And buses, packed above and beyond all reason,
Swayed their ludicrous way towards villages

All over Nepal, enormous arches of bamboo
Rose and bowed to be tied in graceful support
Of the festival swings in every village.

In Chaudaridara, inadequate with a camera,
I sat in awe-struck envy of the young
Cavorting in sprung rhythm above my head.

You want play swing? you asked at the high
Point of every arc inscribing the waiting sky,
And I drew back with a timid, earthbound

No, I'm too old. Children and the cool teens
Eyeing one another laughed. *But for this week,*
You persisted, *old man also can play swing.*

And the gods know I did – the camera has the proof –
While my legs, amazed at themselves, lifted
And pointed towards the light on distant hills.

I give these words to you as *tikka*, in gratitude
For your seven-year-old wisdom, dear Prashant,
Who taught me how to walk the air again.

The Long Dance of Thulo Sybaru

Hoard this: the sheen of starlight on mountains,
As it was and as it will be, here, at the present time.

The name of the village also, hoard it, seeing that
The Long Dance is how it translates, and, look,

See the long procession of summits, step
After step linked in a snowy stateliness,

The reel of stars knocking frosty sparks
From the huge floor of the sky above,

And her own ring whirling around the moon,
As terraced fields step out under her light.

Hoard all this for yourself, and hoard also
The memory of the wedding that welcomed you

Into its own long celebratory dance, when you chanced
By these parts for the first time last year,

And hoard the memory of the young couple anointed
With butter, for prosperity, all through the day.

Hoard this, and hoard the monks chanting, this afternoon,
Sutras for the quiescence of the soul of the newly dead,

While, in the porch, the young lama proudly traced
The wheel of life that flowered by the monastery door.

Traced, especially, those hells whose blacknesses,
In our own deceiving, we conjure from the light.

Hoard, my treasured self, the dawn of each present day
On the darkness you made of the light within yourself.

Hoard your own brightness for the rest of the days of your life,
And the long dance, unbroken, to the very borders of time.

Bridge

May all the gods of Annapurna smile
On the utilitarian soul of the Swiss

Government agency that bored the rock
And sank the stanchions deep to anchor

The cogwheels and the cables that suspend
This most miraculous footbridge that crosses

The awful depth and close-your-eyes tumult
Of the Marsyangdi churning down the gorge.

And may they bless the nut-and-bolted strength
That has replaced the crafted, spare elegance

Of the lovely rope-and-bamboo bridge that sags
Alongside me, as I edge like a second hand

Across the dull, precisely engineered arc
That spans the timeless chaos below.

Safe Passage

Dear Mother, since that the lodge's radiophone
(The first one coming from the high altitudes)
Crackled with that time-lapse in the voice
That you are without doubt dying; and since
That if there is no cloud the helicopter
Will come for us at first light for Kathmandu
And God knows through where else to home,
And the sky is now a hushed dome of stars;
Since that I left before all clouds had cleared
And since that, after all, we may not make it,
What can I do this sleepless night but cling
To the throwaway kindness of the lodge-owner:
When is big trouble, is no need to tell sorry,
And pray safe passage for you and for us all.

Email

for Ang Wong Chhu Sherpa

I would not, in the same breath, join email
With serene, but on my screen your message
Breathes equanimity, and I am touched
By your condolences, and I will honour
Your request to *please don't make bad feelings,*
Your prayer *that her soul will be getting Nirvana.*
I finger the texture of your words as I fingered
The texture of the lama scarf you draped
In sad benediction around my shoulders,
A moment before the shuddering helicopter
Gathered itself, and lifted up to drop
Abruptly from that terrace near Annapurna,
To veer dizzily towards my mother's deathbed.
And so, my guide, my friend, I join my hands
Then touch the keys in *namaste* to you.

At Gosainkunde

There are no two ways
About nightfall: between
One moment and the next
It darkens and freezes,

As the heart might freeze
And darken on itself,
Were it to range only
Among the high places.

Sunrise unlocks the air
Abruptly, as Shiva's trident
Once shattered the glacier
Into a lake's fullness,

Under an admiring sun
That draws from the water
Reflected serrations
Edging against the sky.

At the prayer-flagged pass
Beyond the holy lake,
Unambiguously, the wind
Razors the stony trail

That leads precipitately,
With something like gratitude,
At the end of the day,
Down through misted forest

To houses and terraced fields,
Where straying water-buffalo
Low in the encroaching dark
Among patches of lamplight,

And the heart wavers
Between this warm udder-world
And the clarity of the light,
Above all, at Gosainkunde.

On Thorung La

I had a rucksack of tropes for this poem,
Neatly packed, to be used at the highest point
Of this fortieth anniversary adventure of our lives,
Trekking the whole circuit of Annapurna.

The poem, I knew, would be all achievement,
All epiphany, side by side and step
By exultant step to eighteen thousand feet,
Just the height, I thought, of forty years.

But at Thorung La, as head-torches
Zigzagged painfully up the pitch-dark trail
(*Thorung* meaning *early rising* and so safety
Insisting on an early start for the ascent)

Tropes fell away abruptly into the void
As altitude and gradient sucked the air
From panicking lungs and dragged at boots
While fear waited to fill the vacuum.

Then the inrush – the *inspiration* – of love
Embracing frailty, love that could only gasp
Are you – okay – yes I'm – okay –are you
But knew also that it would trudge its way

To the high pass and down to the next valley
(And in between, and in between, yes,
Those impossible gleaming heights made possible)
Where we could wonder at ourselves again.

And as the poem's idea surged into the poem,
I recalled how long ago the idea of love,
Early and afraid, surged into love itself,
Its urgent, endless plodding towards exhilaration.

In the temple of the low ground, I burn
Incense for our journey, and give thanks
Among the crops and herds, that you and I
Have walked, and known, the altitudes of love.

III

My Lord Buddha of Carraig Éanna

It's to keep the bay level, I joked,
As I nudged him into balance
At the edge of the cliff, his bland
Garden-centre smile facing out to sea

And to Carraig Éanna, its silhouetted
Birds, and its occasional almost-strain
Of old stories recounting themselves
Among the indifferent heads of seals.

He has settled in well. Some two
Or three winters. Stirs himself only
For the approaching lawnmower, sinks
Easily back into where he was.

Two or three winters. Storms foreseen
And unforeseen. The moulded folds
Of his robe bear hints of lichen.
The smile is softened by weathering.

From my window, his shape in the light
Of where he is between sea and sky,
Between field and shore, assumes
Today that he has been here forever.

Equanimity, now and again. Equilibrium.
O My Lord Buddha of Carraig Éanna,
Your plaster-cast presence is welcome,
Rooted in all this betwixt and between!

Buddha and the Pheasant

We hold our breath, dead still in wonder
As the cock pheasant emerges from the shadow

Of the hedge, processing across the cut grass
Towards the edge of the cliff. And just when

He passes by the Buddha who keeps the bay level,
The morning sun catches his puffed-up feathers,

Burnishing the russet breast to a magnificence
Worthy of Achilles' shield, arraying him

From head to tail in gilded armour. O grant him
Many such mornings to preen and strut his stuff

Between this and the other shadow! Here and now
We thank this day for this enlightenment.

Buddha Contemplates his Location

It's not really a cliff, is it? It's just a clay
And rock barrier dumped here by a glacier
Ages ago, when it was taken aback by the sea.

Coincidences of wind and moon and wave
Erode it, infinitesimally or in abrupt collapses
As their moods take them. I cry for myself

Elsewhere, carved on inland mountain cliffs,
My resignation and serenity chiselled deep.
Now I sit here, at the edge, and I am afraid.

Buddha's Places of Birth

Is this the one you brought back from Nepal?
In a rucksack? My half-metre Buddha watched
The sea without comment. *No, Cahersiveen.*
A garden centre. He's plaster-cast, I'm afraid,
And mass-produced. In Germany, I think.
Deflation, disappointment hung in the air.
Awesome, isn't it?, interjected Buddha silently.
I mean, like, I find myself all over the place.
Just about here, there and everywhere.

Buddha Considers the Baraois

The *baraois*, they tell me it's called here,
Or used to be called, the sudden gleam

Of mackerel shoaling under a full moon.
A phosphorescent swelling. There, then gone.

Used to be called, they say, because now
There are no fishermen watching for signs

And there's nobody now, they tell me,
Who walks the cliff at night and knows

How to look for it, or even knows the word.
And I think of those high places I have been

Where nobody now listens for, or knows
The word for that tiny flow of meltwater

From the slope above, that means the snow leopard
Has paused awhile, and silently passed by.

Buddha Considers the Coastguard Station

Silhouetted on a ridge, the coastguard station
Across the bay keeps ruined, roofless watch.

Napoleon, two centuries ago. Rumours of invasion.
A flurry of fortification up and down the coast.

Empty within a decade, it holds no memory now
Of the other stations, of signal-fires and semaphores.

All of this is of no matter: a ruin on the periphery
Of my unblinking vision, of my emptied mind.

Buddha Considers the Tides

This is the tide's way, the moon's silver
Pathway from the seaweed undulating below
To the horizon far out beyond the bay.

And who is to say that it does not rise
To sing its way home through the stars and rest
In the moon's own embrace? The periwinkle

In its blind openings and closings knows it,
And the crab that angles its way between rocks
Feels it in the touch of the light on its shell.

I hear it in the bubbling calls of nightbirds feeding
Between tide-lines, and something in me expands
To encompass all these inchings. These infinities.

Buddha and Amergin

It was, they tell me, just here below,
On the sand and shingle whose tang
Has entered my pores, that Amergin
Beached, and stepped ashore and sang
The beginning of the story. Just about
The time, they say, my own story began
Far away under a far inland tree. The words
Of his beginning have also entered my pores:

Am gaeth i m-muir   *Am wind on sea*
Am tond trethan   *Am wave swelling*
Am fuaim mara   *Am ocean's voice*
Am dam secht ndirend   *Am seven-horned stag*
Am seig i n-aill   *Am falcon on cliff*
Am der greine   *Am sunlit dewdrop*

And so much more. I recite them to myself here
On the cliff-top, easing myself into the place,
The place into me. Sea. Shoreline. Mountains.
The lake, just inland. All the growth, the loss.
The comings and goings. Stories voiced and unvoiced.

How that *Am* exhales itself as my familiar *Om*
From every grain rock and drop and leaf around
And echoes across the bay between headlands!
Words swell up as water swells in the bay
Rebirth   Recreation   Reincarnation   Renewal
And collapse as waves under their own weight.
Words are water discovering its own shape. I pour
The words of Amergin votively, tentatively:

Who makes smooth the stony mountain?
Who elucidates the lives of the moon?
Who proclaims where the sun will rest?

I could live with those words. Many times. Over
And over again I could live with those words.

IV

Entrance

for John F. Deane

Was this, a poet asked from afar,
God's city, the pleroma? And yes, yes,
That otherwordly plenitude lives here,
Infusing pavements and oratories and cells
With the numinosum they aspired to.
Here stone expands with more than it encloses,
Embodies horizons that widen like ripples.

But here too is this world's proclamation:
Marvel at these bouldered walls as you bend
Beneath the huge lintel of the entrance.
Know your own fragility as you climb each
Step towards entry into this citadel.
Know that herein only lies your safety,
Subjecting your self to the Self of God.

And here is Holy Rule and Inquisition
Inherent beneath the weight of stone.
Here is plenitude codified, here are chains
And edicts: here, also, is the triumph of fear.

Puffins

JUNE

You know those pictures:
Kaleidoscopic beakfuls
Of silvery sprat.

That comical look,
The ludicrous, buzzing flight
To hungry burrows.

We've all caught them
Angling their quizzical heads
For our cameras.

AUGUST

Fledglings hatched late starve
When the colony migrates,
Clowning abandoned.

Some downy bundles,
Left behind every year,
Stagger on the rock.

Photograph this too,
The black and white behind all
The rainbow colours.

East Steps

for Peter Marinker

From Blind Man's Cove,
The stone stairway ascends
Steeply, turning and twisting
On itself with the lie
Of the land, until it is
A great snake scaling
The heights, insinuating
Itself into the island
As, in a medieval painting,
A snake insidiously
Contours itself around
A paradisiacal tree,
Its scales the texture
Of leaf and bark,
Its eyes the only
Signifiers of intent.

But does the snake foresee
That, at the summit,
In the citadel hidden
Behind the towering wall
And huge barred door,
Michael the Archangel prepares
His armour of revelation
To dazzle the eye and daze
The suspicious heart, sharpens
A sword that will sever doubt,
And raises to his lips a trumpet
To sound the destruction of evil?

49

But who can foresee
How Michael and the snake
Will shed their armour
And their skin, meld
Each into the other,
Wrestling indistinguishably
Up and down the crags,
Angel into monster,
Knight into suicide bomber,
Custodian into terrorist,
As each new zigzag, every
Reaffirmation of the absolute
Lie of the land is revealed,
Revelation by revelation?

Illuminated Manuscript

Last night I boiled the young sorrel leaves
I had gathered behind the monastery
In the afternoon, while the wind was rising.
And after supper, I wrote for hours, my pen
And notebook pooled in the gas-lamp's light.
The gale battered my hut all night,
While I worked and while, afterwards,
I slept, happy with what I had written.

And, although there was also tinned food,
Instant coffee, a solar-powered fridge
And mobile phone reception near the helipad,
For *supper*, read *collatio*,
For *hut*: read *cell* or *scriptorium*,
For *pen*, read *quill*,
For *notebook*, read *vellum*,
For *gas-lamp*, read *rush-light*,
For *pooled*: read *illuminated*.
And for *happy with what I had written*,
Read, with all due resistance,
Ad majorem Dei gloriam.

Skellig Birds

PUFFIN
Hilarious, yes,
But that sad clown spends winters
Completely at sea.

FULMAR
Looks like the others
But it spits independence
And will not be gulled.

SHEARWATER
Those aerobatics,
Skimming the froth off the waves,
Live up to its name.

PEREGRINE
When its tapered wings
Stir to plunge from the high ledge
Fledgling hearts plummet

ROCK PIPITS
They're grey against stone
But they cheep and wag their tails,
Mad for attention.

CHOUGHS
Shrieking a *cancan*
They display their scarlet legs
To the whole wide world.

PIGEONS
Sometimes they arrive,
Lost souls looking for a new
Sense of direction.

COMMON GULL
For that epithet
The red spot on its beak glows
With indignation.

KITTIWAKES
At Blind Man's Cove
They scream their names loud enough
To waken the dead.

GUILLEMOT
Ridiculous name,
But it's what the guide-book says,
There, in black and white.

CORMORANTS
Totally immersed,
They yearn for a christening
Other than *sea-hag*.

STORM PETRELS
Holed up in stone walls
Warmly safe from the world's storms,
You hear them gurgle.

GANNETS
Wheeling in sunlight,
On those glorious white wings –
What is left to say?

Meditation Terrace, South Peak

It's nothing really, and everything,
Once you grasp the lightness
Of stone in air; once you see
Between the great layers of rock
A seam of white quartz aching
For release into the sunlight;
Once you choose your terrace
Or have it choose itself, in a pause
Halfway to the summit, hanging
High over the drop of the cliff;
Once you hammer and chisel
(here's the strain, here's the groaning)
And lever off the weight of slate slabs
To discover the gleam of your floor,
It's grain urgent with light and air;
Once you gather your slate fragments
(how easy this is, how easy!)
To build the low wall that contains
Your small terrace, so that, kneeling,
You see nothing of the whole island,
Nothing at all of what is behind you,
But are wrapped, if the light is right,
In a seamless, blue robe of sea and sky:
That's all it is, all it is, everything,
Quarrying, construction, the whole thing.

Climbing The Eye of the Needle, South Peak

for Alan Hayden

The Needle's Eye, already well threaded
With safety-ropes, opened like a sleeve
Above us. Could I pull myself through,
Draw the world inside out and discover
The light beyond, like that long ago child
Daring the darkness of his huge pullover?
The sea, dizzily beneath us, heaved disbelief.

Here was the *hand over hand over foothold*
To God I'd written achingly about. Now I recall
Only the coming up and out, the sunlit terrace
Trembling all over in the windy brightness,
And my whole self slipping easily through,
Some old saint's arm giving its reliquary
The slip, punching the air with delight.

Stormbound

The fourth day running now
Without any sign of a boat,
And, ignoring the slap and thump
Of the wind, I stroll to the landing,
Wondering idly about a boat
Tomorrow. A young fulmar
Flaps, and spits straight at me
Its terror of being abandoned.
Then around the last sheltered
Bend above the pier I gape
At a sea that's gone out of its mind.

This is no swell, or tide,
Or crest, or trough or backwash
Ordained by moon and wind.
This is a charge, a hurtling,
A trampling, a goring, a huge
Grey and green and white bulk
Buckling, a frenzy to withdraw,
Heave breath, rear, re-gather
Itself, again, for the great collapse
Again, of itself and of cliffs
And of pier and of everything
Under the sun and moon and stars.

And all at once this raw, tormented air,
This roadway pounded by the knowledge
Of its own pitiful, tenuous hold,
This onlooker, aghast once again
At what he has always known,
Are all urgent with the need

For the stone steps' passage
To the high oratories and cells,
For ordained hours, for bells and ritual
That might placate the implacable,
For the final, clear word upon this rock.

Oratory, South Peak

To place broad slabs across the air
Of a sheer gully, and to wedge,
Just, their sides into its walls –
Is this to form a church floor, clinging
To this peak that urges itself skywards;
Is this, in truth, a rock to build upon?

To know that what you see is not possible
And still to see, and still to stand upon
That whole impossibility set in stone –
Is this what faith means, is this the leap
Into the unknown you know is safe
Because the abyss is more impossible?

And the cisterns hollowed into the rock
That feed rainwater one into the other
When the rain runs from the face of the rock –
Is this the baptism of self in others, whose cells
Across the void, beyond Christ's Saddle
Huddle close together on the other summit?

To touch these stones that were once,
God knows why and when, corbelled
Over a lintel now fallen across a doorway –
Is this to know that questions beyond questions
Collapse back into the shape of themselves,
That the end of questioning is never to answer?

Of Time and Tide

Skellig grew ethereal in our wake
As stone became shimmer in the heat.
But the gravestones in the high monastery
Wedged themselves still in the open earth
Of memory, their shadows reflecting
On the low-tide harbour where we landed
And climbed the iron ladder to the pier.
So much for the evening to reflect on:
Such distances in time, such tides.
And then, next day, to London, over

And back, to a funeral, to attend all
The ceremonies and return to the exact
Hour in the time it takes from one
Full tide to another. And I still cannot
Fathom it, nor take the measure of a span
When no man waits for time or tide
Nor takes note of his shadowself
Straggling in his wake, falling farther
And all the time farther behind, behind
Time itself, and stranded between tides.

The Dragons and Archangels
of Skellig Michael

for Marie Heaney

We knew the race was coming from Galway
And had seen the sails high out to windward,
But a sharp northwesterly had edged us away
To the sheltered road between the lighthouses.

And so it was that Seal Cove all at once
Held its breath when that emblazoned sail,
Familiar from the otherworld of television,
Flared out of the west, waking the sunset.

Here was a presence wonderful beyond belief:
Here was communion, a congregation,
As if the Archangel Michael had abandoned
His solitary, high-peaked wrestling with monsters

For the time being, to descend and watch
That slanted, billowing exuberance burst
Into and out of our vision, to hear your daughter
In your excited phone speak from afar

And invoke *the blessing of the Green Dragon*
On all of us, on the guides high as kites,
On the beaming lighthouse-men, on the twilight
Replete with a grace proper to archangels.

v

January

That is no season for the margins, the thin
Forlorn cries of seabirds along an empty shore,
The exhausted light turning a haggard face
To the overwhelming clouds, and the sodden clay
Of the retreating cliff falling in dribs and drabs.

I will go inland awhile, accept the shelter of woods,
The texture of bark and knotted twigs, will ease
Myself into the dark of leaf-mould, nut-mast,
And become familiar with warm, hidden stirrings
Among the blind, white protuberances of bulbs.

Waiting

When fog freezes heart's landscape
And stops the veins and wells, and drains
The colour from everything that grows,

Oh then heart must kernel its sweet self
In hiding from the hooded crow, and wait
For hints of sap. Then thaw. Then flow.

Tree Hugger

A frosty April morning. The field is lined
With birch and willow, rhyming my meditation
With textured bark, the crystal blue behind
Translucent leaves – the grain, the light –
As I embrace fragility, regeneration.

Talbot Grove, 26 April 2007

05:40

You're only gone to Dingle, overnight
That's all, but the abrupt gale-driven sleet
On the window hammers that absence home
When you make no shape against the clock's
Lit figures, and I cannot smell your hair.

Awake now, reassured, I click the luxury
Of an undisturbing bedside light to read,
And to lever out the nail that drove
Itself slyly home, that other – at sixty,
It does cross the mind – utter absence.

At the Blueberry Barrens of Maine

Blueberry *Barons*, I misheard,
And I imagined dark men
Oozing power and greed.

But the barrens were just an expanse
Of fields in the cleared forest,
Russet and purple after winter snow.

Blueberries in Greenland, remember?
Their powdery skin swollen with juice,
In that lovely, fragile summer.

Across the expanse of the Atlantic,
Well south of the floating ice,
I tender you their memory.

Five Haiku at Chokusi-Mon, Kew Gardens

Away from home
Not completely by myself
But not complete.

Narrow paths unscroll
The curls and spikes of strange leaves:
Pure calligraphy.

Knowing it's water
Gravel ripples under a breeze
That knows its water.

No panel to tell
If the larch is Japanese.
Well, it is now.

In stone lanterns
Hollow centres are unlit
And you are not here.

Flying Home

Having taken unimaginable latitude
With distance, with seasons, we have flown
Northward from solstice into solstice,

From the high, drumming sun of Lesotho
To a pale disc above the horizon. Our plane banks,
And eases through bumpy cloud to Farranfore.

On an even keel again, its retroactive roar
Announces home. We drive to Christmas,
To children, to our anniversary, to our equators.

21 December, 2007

A Good-Morrow to my Wife in New Zealand

The night sky, I know, is different down there
Where you've gone, all that jangle of stars

Resettling themselves. But even up here it now
Seems antipodean. Although I won't fall off,

My world feels upside down, polarities reversed,
And all my equators unbalanced. So come

Back safe and soon, my better hemisphere,
To the sharp north, to the declining west,

Bearing southern balm, bearing eastern light
That will make this old world whole again.

At My Mother's Deathbed

Strange how all the consolatory
Hospital high-tech fades to background
When death begins to assert its shape
On the face on the pillow, and the world
Becomes an open mouth defining itself
As breath or no breath, breath or

No breath. Strange, too, how the light
And dark world of the *piseog* silently
Alights to claim a perch, the one
Against which you always, half-laughing,
Would close your eyes: one solitary magpie,
For sorrow, on the scaffolding outside.

Dog and Waterdog

It hardly knew itself, the beach,
Wide-eyed in the unfamiliar
Sunlit frost that grained the whole
High-up and low-down of it.

And how the banked seaweed
Gleamed fresh at the tide-line,
Redolent of translucent depths
And waving, beckoning mysteries!

Even my golden retriever
Lost the usual run of himself,
Sniffing the air for something
Strange in that huge clarity.

When the seaweed erupted
In a huge flurry of snarling,
It was all stand-off and hackles
Until dog and otter subsided

Into wary curiosity, heads
In sideways sizings up and down.
Then all at once the otter
Streaked undulously to the sea,

And my knight errant, my fool
Of a dog followed, adventurous
To the tip of his streaming tail,
Braving this new otter-world,

Tipping and tilting wildly
At every dive and yards-away
Resurfacing, the otter teasing
Among underwater beams.

Puzzled, he paddled back.
But now that aureate head,
Blazoned on shining, argent sea,
Was touched with otherworldly light.

Heron

The slow parabola of the approaching heron,
The abrupt, almost stalled landing
On reversing wings, then the hunch
Into isolation, all angular concentration.

My dog's intrusion stirs a small dance,
A rise-and-falling hint of flamingo,
Of the grey bird imagining colour
Before it resettles, a few rockpools away.

The tide recovers its ribbed sandbanks.
Now all is latent, all is wait-and-see
And the sun is at its highest, and then
Slowly
      Intently
            The bird
                  Eases
Itself
    Into shimmer, disrobes
                    Itself
Of angles
      And of colours
                Elongates
Itself
    Into the ethereal
               And stabs
        And I
        Am fish
        Am air
        Am tide
        Am light
        Transfixed.

Maine Birds

for Jerry and Carol

On your veranda, elated by the cold
And passion of the dawn, I am reading Frost:
Scatter poems on the floor;
Turn the poet out of door.
The blue jays flickering through the alders
Screech approval, downy woodpeckers
Nod vigorously in affirmation, and geese,
Passing overhead towards Canada, honk
And beat their wings in applause.

Heron Dreams of Becoming Crane

for Phyl Herbert

I am tired of bog, of its grey drizzle,
Of its oozing blackness drawing me down
To its dark heart, below even the horizons
That constrain me. I dream of the beyond.

I dream, especially, when passing over estuaries
Where fresh and salt water commingle
According to the moon's decree. Here is order
Flowing between the bog where I roost

And the rocky shore I fish. My nicknames
Among the peasants – ragged *Nóra Ragaí*,
Scrawny-necked *Jónaí Scrogall* – hurt
My wings into faltering, my flight into leadenness,

Until I dream myself into a looping glide
To where I hunch, dead still, against the light
And free myself into oriental streams of thought
That flow like sunlight over my greyness.

Slowly, my plumage changes. I stretch white wings
In wonder, arrange the rich red-and-black mantle
Below my coronet, and proceed in stateliness
To fly huge distances to where my worth is known.

I pass over secluded roofs and gardens, easing down
To glide by lotus-ponds where scribes and scholars,
Who earlier have gathered for debate and poetry,
Look up, and acknowledge my auspicious passing,

As I soar again, refreshed, towards the far north
And to a high lake where my kind is gathering
For a ceremony where each bird knows its rank,
And I slowly fold my elegant, heraldic wings.

VI

The Howl for Art Ó Laoghaire

(i)
My love holds fast in you!
That day I chanced on you
Beside the market-house,
You were my eye's distraction,
You were my quickened heartbeat,
I left home and family
To travel far with you.

(ii)
It never went bad for me:
You had the parlour cleaned for me,
Rooms painted to please me,
Ovens well-heated for me,
Trout by the gills for me,
Spitted roast meat for me,
Slaughtered beasts for me;
Duck-down sleep for me
Until the cows came home –
Even more, if it pleased me.

(iii)
My firmest friend!
It lives in me always,
That boisterous spring day;
How well it became you,
That gold-banded beaver,
Your silver-hilted sabre
Held in highhanded bravery –
The swaggering, the daring
Had your enemies shaking,
Venomous, but craven;

You ready for a tearaway
On your white-faced mare.
The English abased themselves
Down towards the clay then,
And not for your own sake
But for how much you scared them,
Though you got your grave from them,
My heart's dearest favourite.

(iv)
My chevalier, white-handed!
How well your jewelled tie-pin
Pierced firmly through the cambric,
And the lacing adorned your hat.
When you came from abroad to us
They'd clear the road for you,
And never out of love for you,
But with their deepest curse for you.

(v)
My lover now, and always!
When they come into the hallway,
Conchubhar, everyone's favourite,
And Fear Ó Laoghaire, the small one,
They'll ask, all hot and bothered,
Where I have left their father.
I'll tell them through my horror
He's beyond in Cill na Martar.
They'll call out for their father,
With silence for an answer.

(vi)
My love and my pet!
Kin to Antrim's earl

And to the Barrys from Aolchoill,
A blade well became you
And a gold-banded beaver,
Boots of Spanish leather,
And suits of finest cloth
You had woven abroad.

(vii)
My deepest darling!
I knew nothing of your killing
Until your horse came straggling,
Her reins beneath her trailing
And your blood upon her withers
Back to the figured saddle
Where you'd sit or stand, daredevil.
My first stride cleared the doorstep,
My second flew through the gateposts,
My third step found your stirrup.

(viii)
My wrought hands beating,
I set your mare careering
As fast as ever I've ridden,
To where I found you deathly still
Beside a stunted whin-bush,
Without pope, without bishop,
Without clergy, without priesthood
To read over you from scripture,
Just a woman, old and wizened,
Who spread her cloak to ease you,
And the blood on you still streaming;
Nor did I not stop to clean it,
But palmed it up to drink it.

(ix)
Forever my darling!
Rise up to your full standing
And come away back with me,
That we have a bullock slaughtered,
That we organise a party,
That we get the music started,
That I prepare a bed for you,
With fine sheets spread for you,
And patchwork quilts so heavy for you
They'll make sweat break out in you,
Better than that chill you've taken.

(x)
My firmest, and my favourite one!
There's many a graceful woman
From Cork of the tall sails
To Droichead na Tóime,
With acres of cattle-dowry
And handfuls of gold coin,
Would not have slipped away to lie down
The night that they waked you.

(xi)
My lamb, my sweet one!
Don't ever believe it,
That slander that reached you,
Nor their poisonous sneering
That I had been sleeping.
It wasn't sleep that I needed,
But your children were grieving
And needed me near them,
So I lay down to ease them.

(xii)
You people of my own kind,
Is there a woman in Ireland
Who, night after nightfall,
Would lie down beside him,
Who is carrying his third child,
Who would not lose her mind
When Art Ó Laoghaire is lying
Here, drained and lifeless,
Since yesterday morning?

(xiii)
Morrisín, that I may see you
Disembowelled, bleeding,
Your eyes unseeing,
On your shattered knees –
Who killed my sweet one –
And not one man to be found
Who will shoot you down.

(xiv)
My love and my kind!
Up now, Art, you boyo,
Up on your horse's back,
Away with you to Mágh Cromtha
And back by Inse Geimhleach,
Lowering wine from the flagon –
Because you're indeed your father's son.

(xv)
It's a bitter hurt inside me
That I wasn't beside you
When the bullet was flying,
And I'd take it in my right side

Or the folds of my white blouse,
To let you go for the high ground
You sweet-handed rider.

(xvi)
This I cannot bear –
That I could not be there
When the gunpowder blazed.
Deep, deep in my waist
Or in my dress I'd have taken it
To have let you clean away
To settle with them another day,
Rider of the blue-grey eyes.

(xvii)
My beloved treasure!
It's no hero's reception:
A shroud and a coffin
For the bighearted horseman,
At home by a trout-stream
Or drinking in drawing-rooms
With fashionable women.
And I do not yet comprehend
That all of this has ended.

(xviii)
May you live to know horrors,
Morris , for your foulness!
Who killed the man of my house,
The father of my unborn;
Two children wandering the house,
And in my womb a third
That I'll hardly bring to birth.

(xix)
My shining favourite!
When you headed out the gateway
You turned at once and raced back,
Embraced your two children
And blew a hurried kiss to me.
You said, 'Eibhlín, go quickly
And attend to your business
As soon as ever you can.
I'm going now, and I'm leaving you
And most likely I won't return.'
I only made light of your words,
Having heard them so often before.

(xx)
Dearest friend of mine!
Bright-hilted rider,
Let you rise up now
And attire yourself
In the best of your finery,
Put on your black beaver,
Draw on your calf-hide gloves,
Hold your whip up high;
Your mare is just outside.
Take the eastern by-road
Where trees will quail before you,
Where streams will narrow before you,
Where people will bow before you
If they remember their manners –
A thing sadly out of fashion.

(xxi)
It's not my kin who have gone,
Nor the death of three of my own;

Nor Domhnall Mór Ó Conaill,
Nor Conall whom the tide drowned,
Nor my sister, twenty-six years old,
Who lived high and died young
Among royalty abroad –
It's not these whom I invoke,
But Art to be struck down
Near the river at Carraig an Ime! –
The brown mare's rider
Who lies alone with me here –
Not another living soul near
Only the black-robed women of the mill,
And to multiply my grief,
Their eyes dry of tears.

(xxii)
My calf, my own favourite!
Art Ó Laoghaire,
Son of Conchubhar, son of Céadach,
Son of Laoiseach Ó Laoghaire,
Who came east from the Gaortha
And west from an Caolchnoc,
Where berries are fragrant
And nuts heavy on hazels
And apples cascading
In their proper season.
Who could be amazed now
Were Uíbh Laoghaire to blaze up
With an Guagán's sacred lake
For that skilled horseman's sake,
Who at the end of the chase
Would ride down the failing stag
Beyond the pack's baying?
And oh, you sharp-eyed rider

What happened last night to you?
For I felt deep inside me
The wide world could not strike you
When I laid out your finery.

(xxiii)
My friend and my love!
Kin to noblest bloodlines,
With eighteen women to nurse you,
Whose pay for this was good –
A milking cow, a mare,
A sow and her litter,
A mill by a river,
Gold coins and silver,
Fine velvet and silk,
A farm from the landlord –
For their breasts yielding milk
To the heir of fine manhood.

(xxiv)
My deep, deepest love!
My pet, my whitest dove!
Although I never came to you,
With troops of followers to save you,
That was no shame to me
For they were in a hard place,
In closed-up chambers
And in narrow grave-pits
In a sleep beyond waking.

(xxv)
Were it not for pestilence
And the black death
And foul infection,

That band of hard horsemen
Would be shaking their harness
In clamorous procession
On their way to your burial,
My bighearted Art.

(xxvi)
My love on me shining!
Kin to those wild horsemen
Who would track through the glen
Until you'd turn them again
Back into your dininghall,
Where knives were being sharpened,
Pork served up for carving,
With endless racks of finest lamb
And a mess of oat grain fattening
To speed the horses' galloping –
Sleek long-maned stallions
And grooms standing by them
With no reckoning for lodging
Or for the horses' foddering
From week to week's ending
While you partied with your friends.

(xxvii)
My own calf, my favourite!
I saw through a dark haze
A nightmarish vision,
In Cork in the late hours
Alone where I lay:
That our bright house was razed,
That the Gaortha had dried,
That your hounds had no baying,
That birdsong had died
When you were found lying

Out on the bare hill
Without priest, without cleric,
Just an old, old woman
Who spread a corner of her shawl
On you stitched to the clay there,
My Art Ó Laoghaire,
With your blood cascading
Down your gaping shirt.

(xxviii)
My rooted love!
How well that suited you,
Stockings of toughest stitching,
High-polished knee-boots,
A tricorne Caroline
And a whip to flick at
A frisky colt –
And many a modest maidenly eye
Drank you in from behind

(xxix)
My love for my life!
When you went to the prosperous
And powerful towns,
Those merchants' wives
Would bow right down to you
Because they knew deep inside them
How in bed you would drive them,
No better front-rider
To sire a child for them.

(xxx)
By Jesus Christ, there is nothing,
No headgear, no millinery,
Nor finely-stitched linen,

No shoe, no stocking,
No furniture or hanging,
Not even the brown mare's tackling,
That I won't sell to buy law
And I will travel abroad
To petition at court
And if I get no satisfaction
I will come straight back
To the black-blooded savage
Who rifled my treasure.

(xxxi)
My love and my pet!
If my call were to echo
To Doire Fhionáin westward
And to Ceaplaing of the yellow apples,
It's many the light horseman
And white-kerchiefed woman
Would be here with all speed
To weep by your head,
My laughing Art.

(xxxii)
And my heart is grateful
To the fine women of the mill,
For the tears they have shed now
For the brown mare's fallen rider.

(xxxiii)
May you dearly rue it,
Seán Mac Uaithne!
If it was a bribe you wanted
Why not have come to me
And I'd have given you plenty:

A fine long-maned pony
To have sped you away from
Any crowds or strangers
At the first sign of danger;
I'd have given you cattle,
Or sheep when they're lambing,
I'd have seen you well-suited,
And spurred and booted,
Although it would have stuck
In my craw to have looked at you,
Because according to rumour,
You're a spineless wee boor.

(xxxiv)
White-gloved rider!
Since now you are laid low
Rise up to Baldwin,
Of the scrawny mind
And the scrawny body,
And make him pay dearly
For your beloved mare
And for what I must bear.
May his children never blossom!
To Máire I wish no harm,
Although I do not love her,
But my mother bore her
Three seasons in her womb.

(xxxv)
My love deep, deep down!
Your stacks of barley stand
And your cows' yield is good.
But my heart is in a gloom
That all of Munster could not cure

Nor the smiths of Oileán na bhFionn.
Until Art Ó Laoghaire comes once more
There will be no lifting of the sorrow
That has my heart blocked,
Shut utterly off,
Like a chest still locked,
When the key has been lost.

(xxxvi)
You weeping women, hold
Your step out there as one,
While Art Mac Conchubhair calls a round,
And one more for the poor
Before he enrols in that school –
To learn no lore or tune,
But to bear the clay and stone.

from the Irish of Eilín Dhubh Ní Chonaill
(c.1743 – c.1800)

Lightning Source UK Ltd.
Milton Keynes UK
UKOW051308230412

191297UK00001B/13/P